The Songs of Soul

Poetry By EagleSoulMan

Khan Eagle

The Songs of Soul
Copyright © 2020 by Khan Eagle

All rights reserved. No part of this publication
may be reproduced, distributed, or
transmitted in any form or by any means,
including photocopying, recording, or other
electronic or mechanical methods, without the
prior written permission of the author, except
in the case of brief quotations embodied
in critical reviews and certain other non-
commercial uses permitted by copyright law.

Tellwell Talent
www.tellwell.ca

ISBN
978-0-2288-2176-2 (Hardcover)
978-0-2288-2175-5 (Paperback)
978-0-2288-2177-9 (eBook)

Table of Contents

When You Fall in Love 1
What is Love 2
Love: The Sly Hunter 3
The Secrets of Happiness 4
The Secrets of Success 5
Be Patient 6
Father 7
The Army of Sun 8
Free as Kites 10
What is Freedom 11
Immortal Kingdom 12
Songs of a Sparrow 13
A Word in a Bird 14
The Stranger 15
Hide and Seek 16
Hurricane 17
A Secret Love Story 18
Once Upon Time 19
Reserved Dreams 20
Hope is a Lighthouse 21
Come Like a Storm 22
Notes of the Night 23
The Swan of the Lagoon 24

Wild Orchid	25
Among the Stars	26
Our First Love Song	27
Meet Me Where the Two Seas Meet	28
Fruitless Tree	29
Come to Me Tonight	30
I Could've Forgotten You	31
You Didn't	32
The Storm in Your Looks	33
Living Fall in Mid of Spring	34
Deep Sorrow	35
Don't Lose Your Hope	36
My Inner World	37
Invisible Wings	38
Each Road is a Hope	39
Sugar Over Dose	40
If You Were with Me	41
Wanted	42
The Fire Behind the Light	43
Slopes of Silence	44
Layla and Majnoon	45
For Lovers	46
Time of Owls	47

When You Fall in Love

Flowers talk to you
when you fall in love
Birds sing for you
when you fall in love
Your heart gets wings
Your mind stumbles, sinks
Her voice nonstop rings
when you fall in love
You hear her in every song
You see her in everything
All seasons are spring
when you fall in lOVE

What is Love

"Love is a desert flower"
the old man said:
"It's a rebel, a survivor
It may grow in most adverse
and unfriendly sites
It also has a pride
as all wild flowers do"

"Love is an untamed horse"
said the young man:
"With an irrepressible inner force
it always wants to run and run
chasing only the instinct
without a reason"

Love: The Sly Hunter

"How can we catch love"?
The young man asked:
"You cant catch it
No, you cant"
The old man said:
"It isn't a prey
Its a sly hunter
But;
if you want to be hunted
just pray
and remove your armor
Make your chest
an open target"
"How can I know it when it comes?
The young man asked:
"From the pain in your heart
It never misses"
The old man answered

The Secrets of Happiness

You are asking me about
the secrets of happiness
If you've smelled a rose
without picking it
or helped a needy
unrequited
If you've touched a heart
or patted an orphan child
If you've shared a bread
with a total stranger
Don't ask me sir
Don't kid me please
You know for sure
what happiness is

The Secrets of Success

Once, a young stream asked an old river
how to reach sea which was her sole desire
The river said its not easy for a tiny body
You have to take a long and thorny journey
You'll face many obstacles on your way
Yet, I'll give you the four keys of success:
Love, struggle, insistence and patience

Be Patient

See how everything waits in its line
to come or to go on the right time
Just like when miracles appear
at the peak point of despair
Just like how rain drops wait
to fall on earth
and the seeds in dirt
count their time
to emerge
to see the sun
Just be patient
Your turn
for sure
will come
sooner
or later

Father

Each line on his forehead has a story
Each wrinkle stands for a deep worry
He is a father striving to earn his bread
working like ants, shedding his sweat
He forgets all his tireness when he is home
As his family says they have missed him
He never expects anything from them
other than happy smiles on their faces
and a sweet, heart warming welcome

The Army of Sun

Move away!
Give the way!
The army of Sun is arriving
I hear the soldiers'
thunderous rumbles
which are shaking
earth and heavens
And now i see the cavalries'
glowing foreheads
and the scintillant shoes
of their majestic horses
Send the good news
to the every corner
that the dawn is so near
Sun will rise sooner
The sinister darkness
will look for a hole

to hide it's vile tail
The cold hearts will be warming
The hopes will bloom again
The faded roses in gardens
will joyfully open their eyes
The chicklets which wait mornings
eventually will take their wings
The light will suffocate darkness
What a wonderful news!
The morning is coming to embrace us

Free as Kites

Kites are meant to be free and high
As much as flying birds in the sky
Test your wings, they're ready to fly
Emerge from your ashes again
Reach to new heights as free kites
Inhale the freedom you gain
Now you're free, not bound to any chain
Apart from fears, aware of your might

What is Freedom

If you are sick of boredom
and if you want to know
what is the real freedom
Mountains are calling you
where you can touch clouds
watch the stars from close
listen to the bird's songs
from a shepherd's voice
see the whole world
under your feet
and savor the victory:
The prize of your feat

Immortal Kingdom

Close your eyes
Spread your wings
Lets fly together
to the far places
Let's soar
over the mountains
chasing our
eagle instincts
racing with the wind
inhaling freedom
to the core
hunting joys in the skies
conquering the dreamland
where we've founded
our immortal kingdom

Songs of a Sparrow

She was a delicate daisy
on the verge of a highway
She was always happy
since the sun was smiling her
everyday...
One day the sun has gone
The black clouds invaded the sky
A furious storm hit her at first
Then she was slammed down
by the cruelly falling hail
While she was faded, resentful
and mourning in a deep sorrow
she found her hope, her joy again
with the cheerful songs of a sparrow

A Word in a Bird

I whispered you a magic word
The word turned into a bird
The bird had flied and flied
Then landed on your hand

Open the message by kissing the bird
The bird will turn back into the word
It will be that word only between us
The WORD which will forever last

The Stranger

She was her, "The Stranger"
who brought me the smell of wild flowers
She was her, the "sweet Intruder"
whispering me the loveliest words
Her words were hot breezes of far seas
Her speech was songs of palm trees
Her hair reminded me the monsoon rains
It was so long, so intense and relaxing

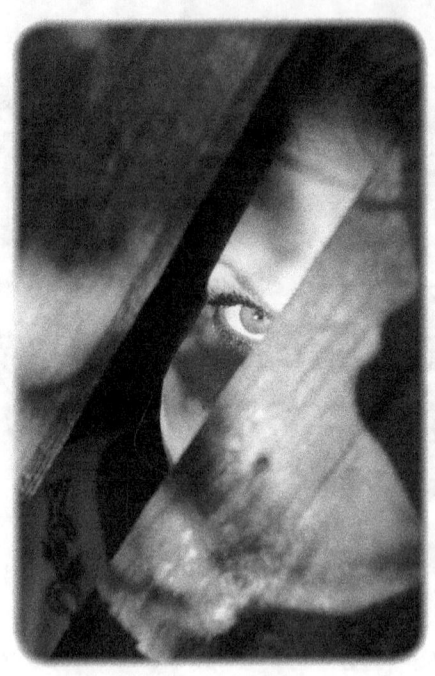

Hide and Seek

Her:
"You're like a sea of mystery
I'm a tiny creek striving to reach thee
While I'm approaching you day by day
As if you're constantly moving away"

Him:
"You're like a shadow of afternoon
I can't catch up, though I chase you
This hide and seek will end soon
I will find and seize you"

Hurricane

She carved his name on her heart
and engraved his image to her brain
She felt him in every heart beat
and recalled him always with pain
Her love was so deep, so insane
But her waiting was just in vain
It wasn't anything in human feat
enchaining an untamed hurricane

A Secret Love Story

As the ocean rests it's restless head
on the tender embrace of the coast
and the sounds of gushing waves
are muted by the solaces of tales
A story fills up the night
A secret love story
in which the Moon chases the Earth
and relentlessly flirts with her
making her various faces
along the way of his phases

Once Upon Time

Once upon time
remember
when spring
was prevailing
on our lives
as everywhere
and melting the ice
on the river
and between us
we were overflowing
just like spring floods

Remember the old juniper tree
we used to visit it daily
and lie on ground
imagining the pink clouds
as heaps of cotton candy

Reserved Dreams

Do you know
how many trains take off from my heart
to carry my immense longing for thee
Have you got any idea
how many birds flap in me
for my silent screams to be heard

I seek your taste in every sip
and in every breath of my sleep
I've reserved all my dreams for you
in a hope that I could encounter you

Hope is a Lighthouse

As the fog aversely leaves
the bosom of mother earth
and disperses towards the skies
a heavy longing replaces it
descending on my heart
and besieging me
from all sides

Hope is a lighthouse in distance
guiding me in a pitch darkness
One day this yearning ends
when you show up among the mists

Come Like a Storm

Come!
All of a sudden, one night
Come in form of a storm
or a thunder if you want
that shakes from the bottom
any single heart...
Come at speed of light
such as the lightning
lashing the ugly face
of the pitch darkness
Or pour on me
like an incessant downpour
Make me soaked with love
down to the core

Notes of the Night

It was a dark, rainy night
HE was writing by a candle light
when the wind flew open the window
when SHE sneaked in like a shadow
HE saw only a dim silhouette
Then, HE felt HER bare feet
on HIS very heart strings
Each step had turned out to be a note
SHE had composed the best love songs
as SHE had kept walking that night

The Swan of the Lagoon

You were a beautiful swan
that used to swim
in the crimson lagoon
which is reddened
by the last kisses
of farewelling sun

You were as expected as
a baby's first words
and as respected as
a dying man's bequests

But I don't know why
All of a sudden one day
You had flied far away
Yet there was something
you had already forgotten:
The lagoon belonged to you
You belonged to the lagoon

Wild Orchid

She is a wild orchid grown in a far terrain
A snowflake; so unique, so pure, so innocent
Even the wind can't dare to touch her silk skin
while combing her hair every morning
Butterflies ask her permission
to have a wander on
Flies stop buzzing,
ants cease working
when they see her
sleeping…

Among the Stars

I am not with you tonight
My love, forgive me please
Yet, don't feel so sad
Go to your balcony
The full moon will be there
As an ambassador of me
bringing warm greetings
hug-full yearnings
sultry, wet kisses
for you, from me
Go to your balcony
I'll be in the skies
watching you
among the stars…

Our First Love Song

Recall the day we held hands in woods
as sun was hiding behind clouds
We'd heard a song rising
It was the rain softly drizzling
Drops had turned into notes
falling on our lips like dots
leaving there ineffable treats
I don't know it lasted for how long
But it was our first love song

Meet Me Where the Two Seas Meet

If you want to find me one day
let your heart be your compass
You'll see rose petals along your way
Follow them, you'll reach me thus

Yet; leave your fears, pride behind
Open the closed curtains of your heart
Leave even your shoes, come to me on bare feet
I'am waiting you where the two seas meet

Fruitless Tree

Your love has grown in me
day by day, year by year
Just like the long journey
of a seed becoming tree
But now I dreadfully fear
that spring could come earlier
An uninvited cold breeze
could catch us unawares
And it would turn our love
into a fruitless tree

Come to Me Tonight

Come to me tonight my love
Come to me all alone
leaving your tears behind
and your fears of any kind
There will be
just you and me
and the old palm tree
with the other few friends:
The moon, the coast and and the sea
only as witnesses
for our holding hands
and giving our oaths

I Could've Forgotten You

I could've forgotten you already
if songs hadn't betrayed me
I could succeed to erase
your charm, your smile, your face
forever from my memory
If sun had ceased smiling at me
I could learn how to survive
without your ravishing scent
if the wind had failed to haul it
almost everyday into my hive

You Didn't

I had written your name on mountains
The blind saw it, bats saw; you did not
I had become water flowing through fountains
Birds drank me, wolves drank; you did not
I had cried out your LOVE to the hard rocks
Deafs heard me, rocks heard; you did not

The Storm in Your Looks

There is no definition of the storm in your looks
Neither i can find it in dictionaries nor in books
The storm that submerges my priceless ships
which are brimmed with my hopes and wishes

Please close your eyes, stop this raging storm
I have done nothing to deserve this scorn
If loving you is a crime, yes I am guilty
Now all i want is a little peace and tranquility

Living Fall in Mid of Spring

Since you have gone without saying a word
Trees have been shedding their leaves
in place of their tears
The flowers, you planted by your own hands
keep mourning after you, not smiling anymore
Even sparrows are resentful, not singing
We are living fall in the mid of spring

Deep Sorrow

Sunk in such a deep sorrow
she's trembling like a wounded sparrow
Her smile is mired down on her lips
Her happiness is detainee in her sadness
She is as silent as falling rime at night
As lonely as abandoned hut in forest
She's faded and lightless such roses
detached from their branches

Don't Lose Your Hope

A sorrow from fall is nestled in your eyes
Your hair is sagged like weary twigs
As if neither nights give you hope nor days
As if the whole world is on your shoulders

This storm calms one day, don't forget!
Fall goes, winter ends, spring returns
The sorrow gives way to the happiness
Just, dont lose your hope, your faith

My Inner World

Come in, take my hand and firmly hold
let me show you my inner world
I've wells filled with the tears of years;
caves, brimmed with orphan fears
Sleepless nights sit on this corner
Restless days stand on the other
That door opens to a small backyard;
where I grow my hopes,
where I console my heart...

Invisible Wings

Don't be afraid the sweetest
Come on! Wipe your tears
Everything has an owner
Don't think you are all alone
There's ointment for wounded hearts
There sure is the One who hears
Don't stand there with broken wings
There are invisible arms and fins
which will hug you
and keep you in blessings

Each Road is a Hope

Don't be so hopeless
Stand up, leave your ropes
There are many hopes
waiting for you, and many roads
Each road is a hope after all
Do not ever forget that
at the beginning of every hope
and at the end of every road
In fact
Everywhere
You could imagine or not
No doubt
HE is there

Sugar Over Dose

While i was running away from all ties
You've become my inevitable addiction
I dont know the number of butterflies
in my stomach and my heart in action

I know, i will die suddenly one day
The diagnosis will be the sugar over dose
Although its so hard, i must run away
Or, you will be my death's cause

If You Were with Me

I would never complain
about the pouring rain
if you were with me now
my pitiless darling

Sun wouldn't set so beautifully
if you hadn't watched it with me
Stars were much closer and brighter
when you were lying my beside
Life is more brutal and harder
Since ever you put me aside

Wanted

Her smile, I have to stress
Her damn warm smiling
must be counted among the causes
which lead to global warming
And her killer eyes must be placed
at the top of the list
that declares
the most wanted killers
And she has to be convicted
not only for her inciting action
but also for having and carrying
weapons of mass destruction

The Fire Behind the Light

I know
your face is the reflection of moonlit
I can't figure it out, yet
from where you have seised
the glow of a dagger in your eyes
I am so afraid that
it will tear me to shreds

No, there is no definition of my feelings
I love you as if I have never loved
You're the sweetest killer of my sleepings
I know there is a fire behind the light
I approach you, yet, I fear to touch

Slopes of Silence

They have clung to the slopes of silence
afraid of falling into the attraction of fire
just like the butterflies around the lights
and scared of getting stuck in a mire
Yet, hearts were beating for each other
They could avoid growing yearnings
if it was possible to reign dreams

Layla and Majnoon

Layla:

O Majnoon!
What has dragged you to the deserts?
What did you find in your long solitude?
Have you heard of my silent screams?
Have you felt my lonely tears?

Majnoon:

O Layla!
I heard you in whines of the wind
I felt that you are crying
when it started to rain
I found you there
in everything

For Lovers

Although you are a scar in my heart
I don't want to get healed
Your name is on my forehead
eternally sealed

All I need
in this greedy world
can be summed up in two:
Just a little oxygen
more from You
And my pray is sole
"O! God
Cut my air first
before taking her soul"

Time of Owls

The silence of the Poet
was not for nothing
It was almost night
Owls were awaiting
Time was up for nightingale
Owls would tell another tale
Roses pulled their curtains
Birds scurried to their nests
It was time for the darkness
in which
only the hoots of owls
could prevail

www.ingramcontent.com/pod-product-compliance
Lightning Source LLC
LaVergne TN
LVHW021740060526
838200LV00052B/3382